AF426423

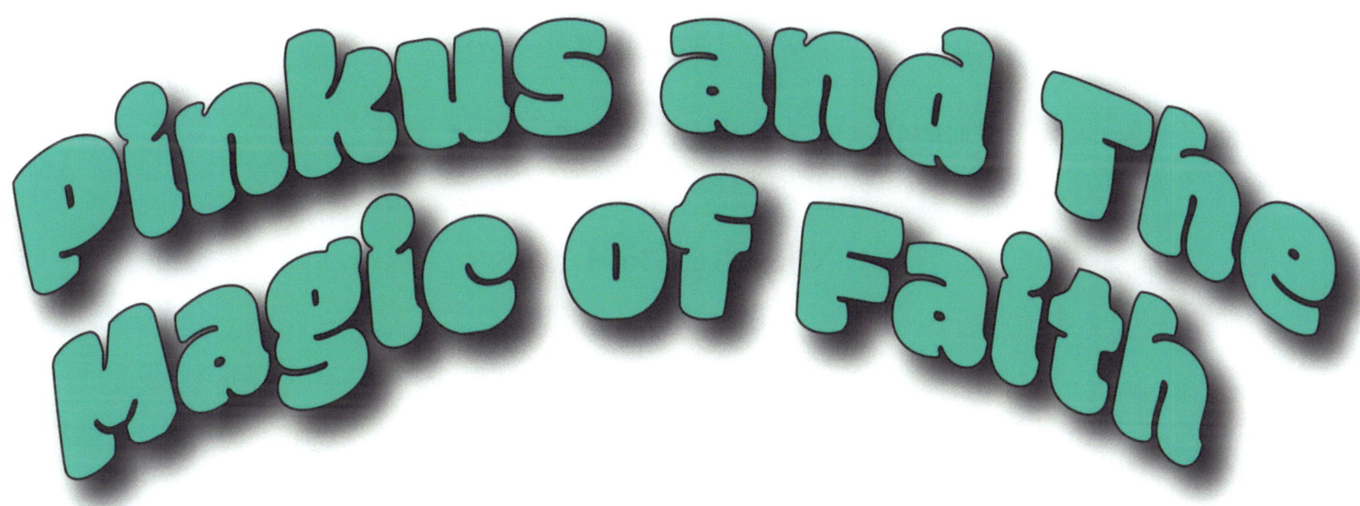

Pinkus and The
Magic of Faith

PINKUS AND THE MAGIC OF FAITH
by Ingrid Honkala, PhD

DESIGNED & ILLUSTRATED BY
Faby G.H.

Published by the author in collaboration with Fearless Literary Services
www.ingridhonkala.com

ISBN: 979-8-9916843-1-6

PROJECT PRODUCTION & MANAGEMENT:
D. Patrick Miller • Fearless Literary Services
www.fearlessbooks.com/Literary.html

Pinkus and The Magic of Faith

Who Is Pinkus?

Hi there! My name is Ingrid, but when I was a little girl,
my mom used to call me Pinkus.
The story I'm about to share with you is a true one!

Ever since I was small, I could talk to animals,
plants, and even angels.

These angels were so beautiful, glowing in all sorts
of colors. They helped me see that we are all special,
and inside, our souls shine like bright, pure light.

They also taught me something really important:
we are never alone,
and when we fill our hearts with love and say,
"thank you," amazing things can happen!

Hi! I'm Pinkus!

I come from a country called Colombia,
and I grew up in a big, busy city called Bogotá.

2

Our house had a big patio right next to the room I shared with my sisters. I often saw little creatures like spiders and slugs crawling around the patio.

HOUSE
7
MAILBOX

When my baby sister was born, my parents thought our house was getting too small, so they decided to build a new bedroom for all of us to fit comfortably.

The baby slept in my parents' room
until she was seven months old.
Then, they decided to use part of
the patio to build the new bedroom.

6

Sorry!
WE ARE UNDER
CONSTRUCTION
coming soon!

But something strange happened
while they were building
the new room-slugs started
coming into OUR bedroom!

9

And to my surprise,
they crawled right into my bed because
it was the closest to the door!
wiiiiiiii
wiiiiiiii

10

Pinkus
LOVE

LiLi
L O V E
LiS
L O V E
12

Almost every night,
I would find slugs hiding
in my sheets when I
went to bed!

13

So, every night, my mom and
I would check my bed, just
to make sure no sneaky slugs
were hiding there!

But sometimes, even after checking, I'd wake up in the middle of the night with slimy slugs crawling on me! Feeling scared, I would call for my mom to help.

16

Even though I was scared, I really loved and respected animals. So, I would ask my mom to help me gently take the slugs back to the patio without hurting them.

18

One night, after we checked
my bed like we always did,
I asked my mom,

19

?
?
?
"Why is this happening
to me?"
20

Feeling my sadness,
she hugged me tight
and said,

"Do you remember
when I told you
that praying and
asking with faith is
the same thing?"

21

"Yes Mom, I remember," I replied.

Mom said,
"Then, talk to the slugs. Tell them
you love them, but you'd rather
they don't come into your bed anymore.
Let them know they don't belong there."

After a little pause, she added,
"Have faith and be patient—it might
take some time to convince the slugs."

You don't belong here
24

Believing in my mom's words,
I talked to the slugs, sure they
could hear me. Every night, while
kneeling by my bed and saying my
prayers to God and the angels,
I whispered:

25

"Little slugs,
I love you, but you belong on the patio,
not in my bed. With all my heart,
I ask you to stay outside.
I promise I'll keep protecting you
and visiting you there."

26

28

I repeated these words every night for several days. Then one day, I saw the angels smiling, and the slugs were gone.

30

After not seeing slugs on my bed
for several days,
I was overjoyed with happiness.

32

Filled with joy, we celebrated by
hugging each other, my sisters and I,
33 and thanking the angels and God.

Since I had started listening to the
angels when I was only 4 years old,
I remembered something they always
told me as my mom was leaving
the bedroom:

"Everything is alright."

34

I giggled and shouted to my mom,

"Having faith is when you know that everything will be alright, Mommy?"

35

"It's kind of like that,"
she replied with a smile.

"You put things in God's hands
and trust that they will be fixed.
You just have to believe
and work for it."

36

Once my mom left the bedroom,
I excitedly whispered to
the angels and God,

"The slugs listened!"

Then I heard the angels gently
say, "Of course they did. When you
hold God in your heart, there is
only one language...

That's how, at the age of six,
I learned there was real power in
praying and in this mysterious thing
everyone called

"faith."

From then on, I began to pray every
day for the well-being of my family,
the angels, all people, and animals in
the world.

38

Here is Pinkus when she
was three years old!

Acknowledgments

A heartfelt thank you to my wonderful mom
for her love, wisdom, and faith, which have
guided me throughout my life.
Your support has been invaluable.

To my dear sister Faby, your beautiful illustrations
have brought this story to life. Thank you
for making our book shine with your creativity.

I also extend my gratitude to the angels
for their loving presence and inspiration.

And to my family, thank you for your
endless love and encouragement.

With all my love and profound appreciation,

Ingrid

www.ingramcontent.com/pod-product-compliance
Lightning Source LLC
Chambersburg PA
CBHW042125150726
48005CB00029B/300